MY PETS COLORING BOOK

For Children - Learn as you Color

By Gindan Media

Amazon.com

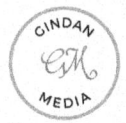

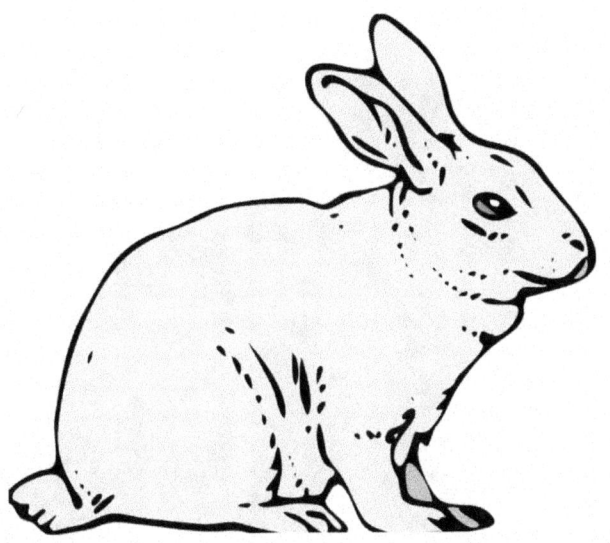

Rabbit

● RED

● YELLOW

● BLACK

Color the
rabbit with
these colors

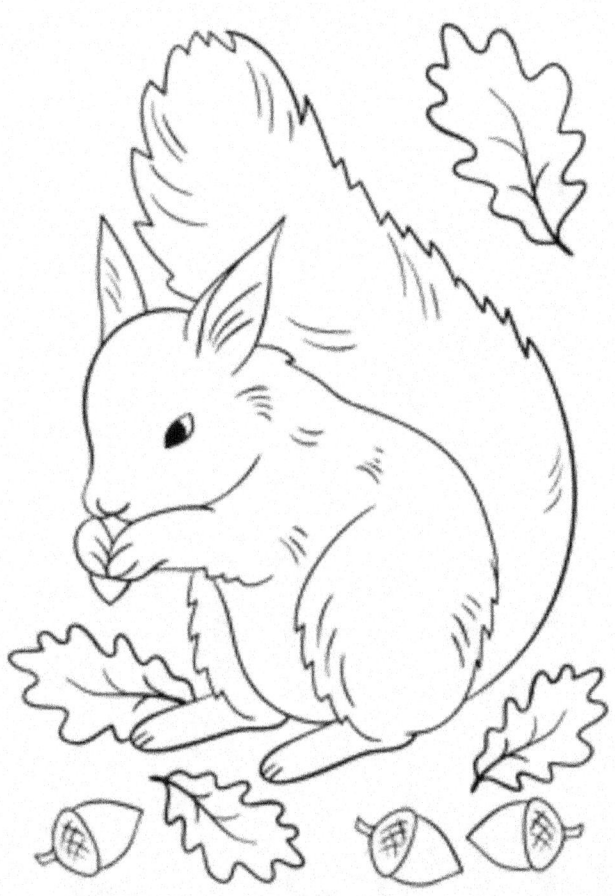

Squirrel

- Orange
- Yellow
- Green

Color the
Sqirrel with
these colors

GINDAN MEDIA

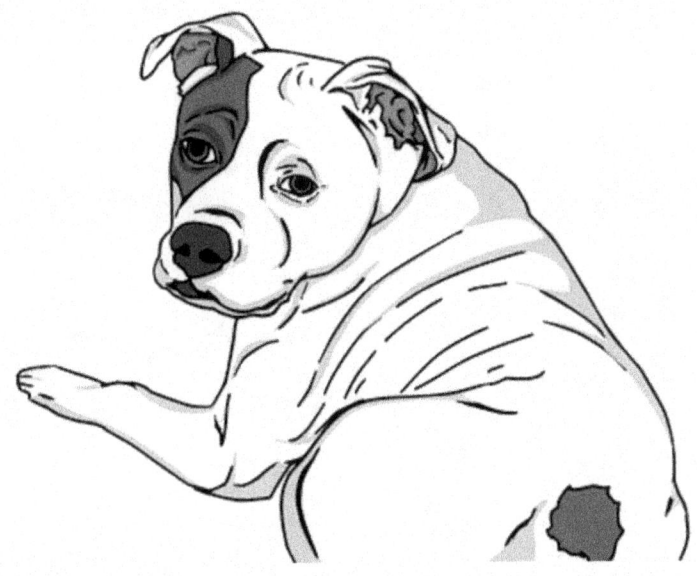

Dog

● Brown

● Black

● Yellow

Color the Dog
with these
colors

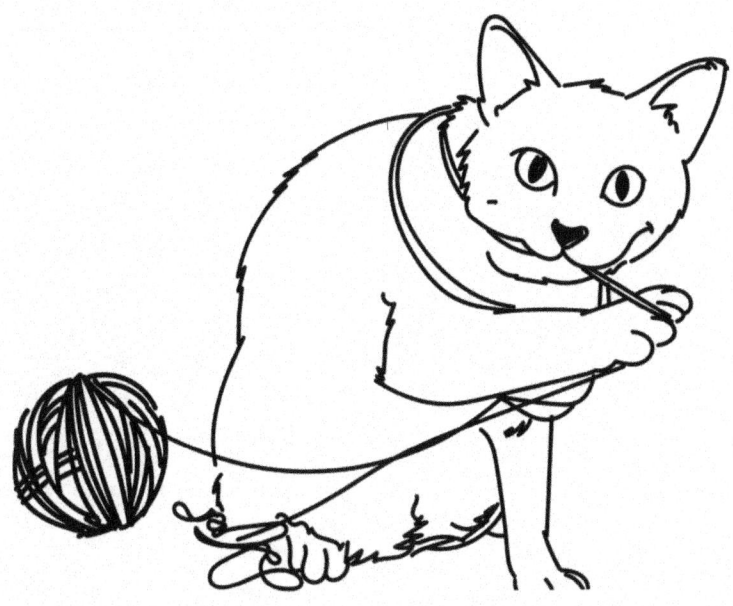

Cat

● Blue

● Pink

● Yellow

Color the Cat
with these
colors

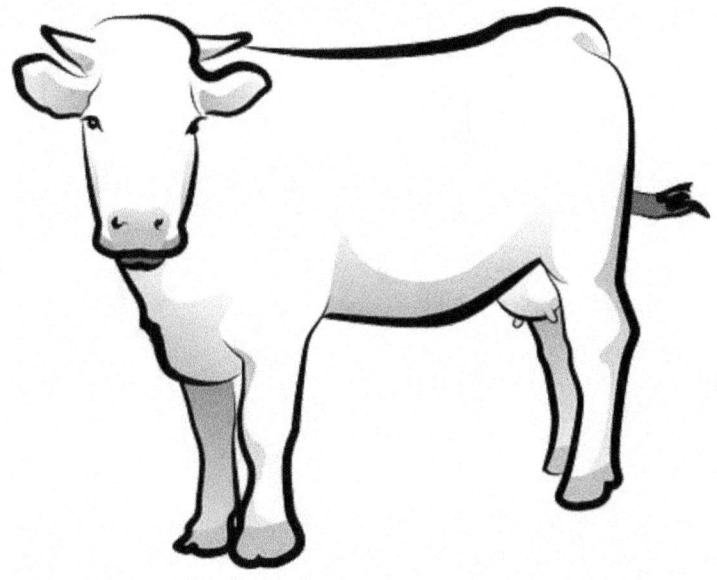

Cow

Blue

Pink

Yellow

Color the Cow
with these
colors

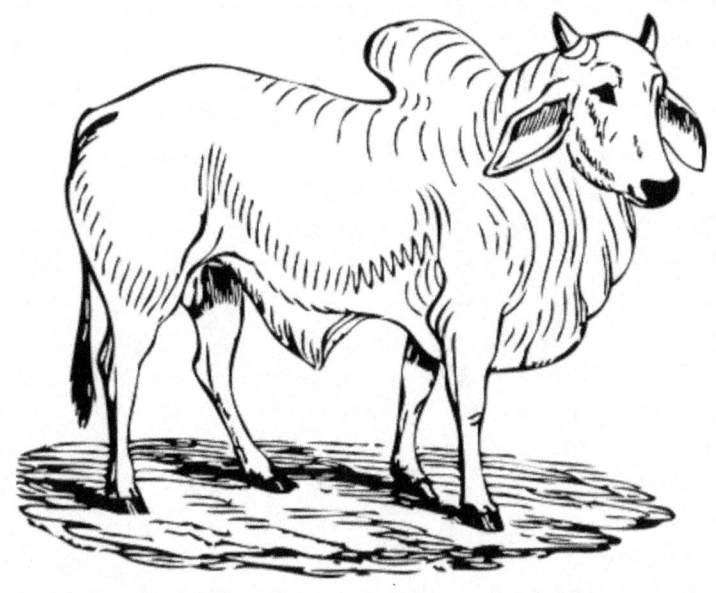

Bull

● Black

○ White

● Orange

Color the Bull
with these
colors

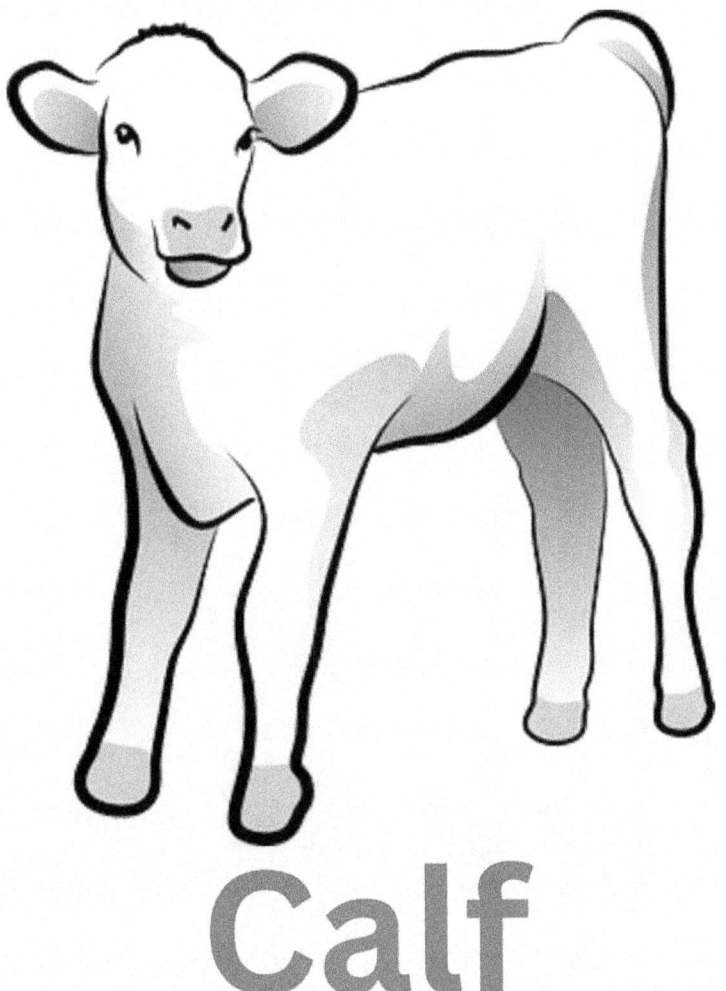

Calf

Lite Blue

Yellow

Brown

Color the Calf
with these
colors

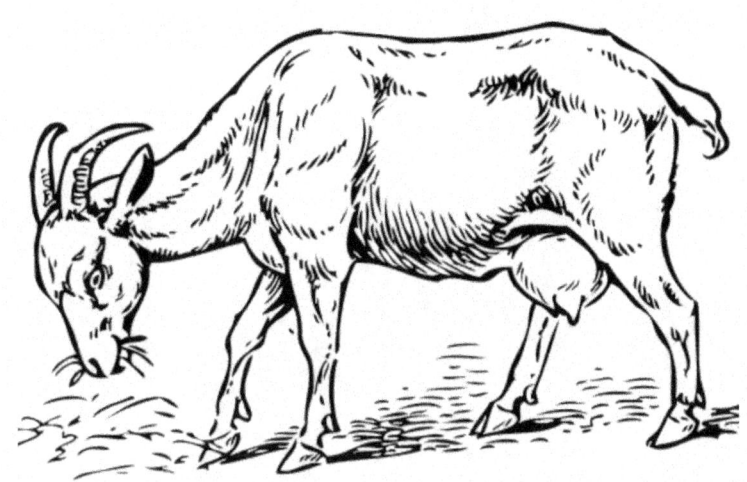

Goat

Pink

Yellow

Green

Color the Goat
with these
colors

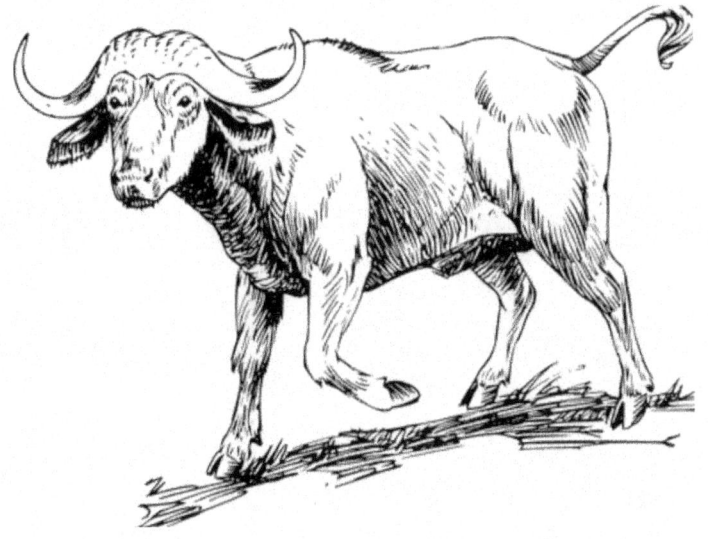

Buffallo

● Black

○ White

● Green

Color the
Baffallo with
these colors

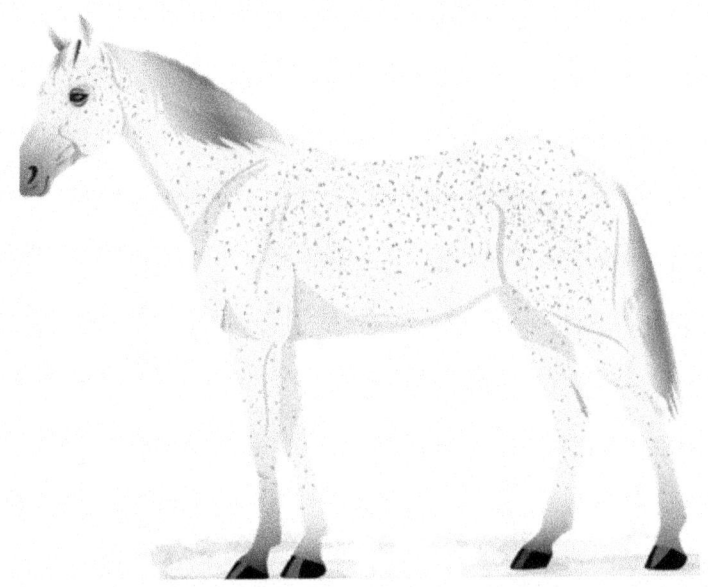

Horse

⬤ Orange

⬤ Grey

⬤ Yellow

Color the Horse
with these
colors

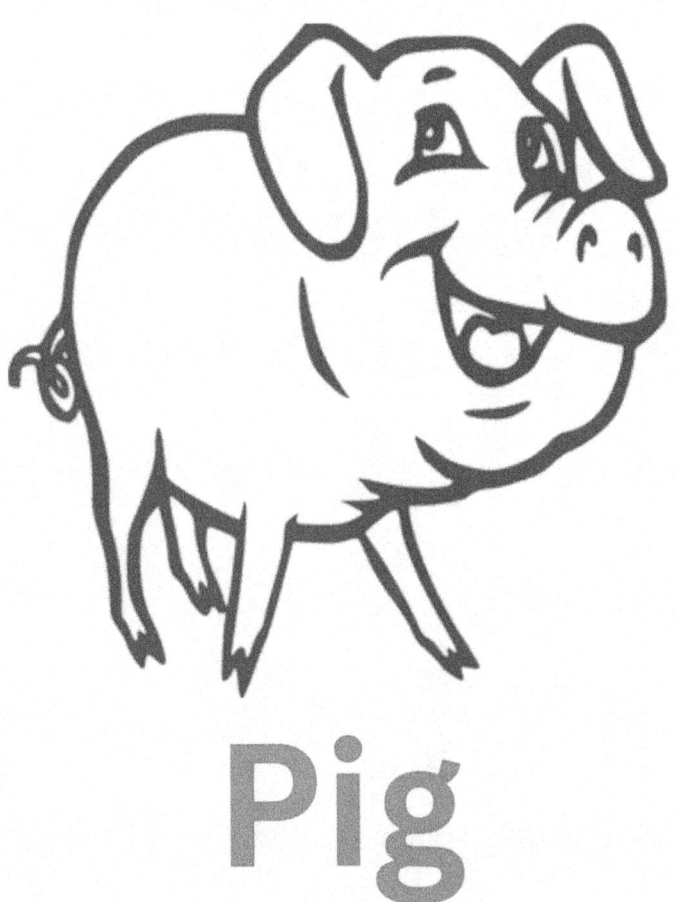

Pig

● Pink

● Blue

○ Yellow

Color the Pig with these colors

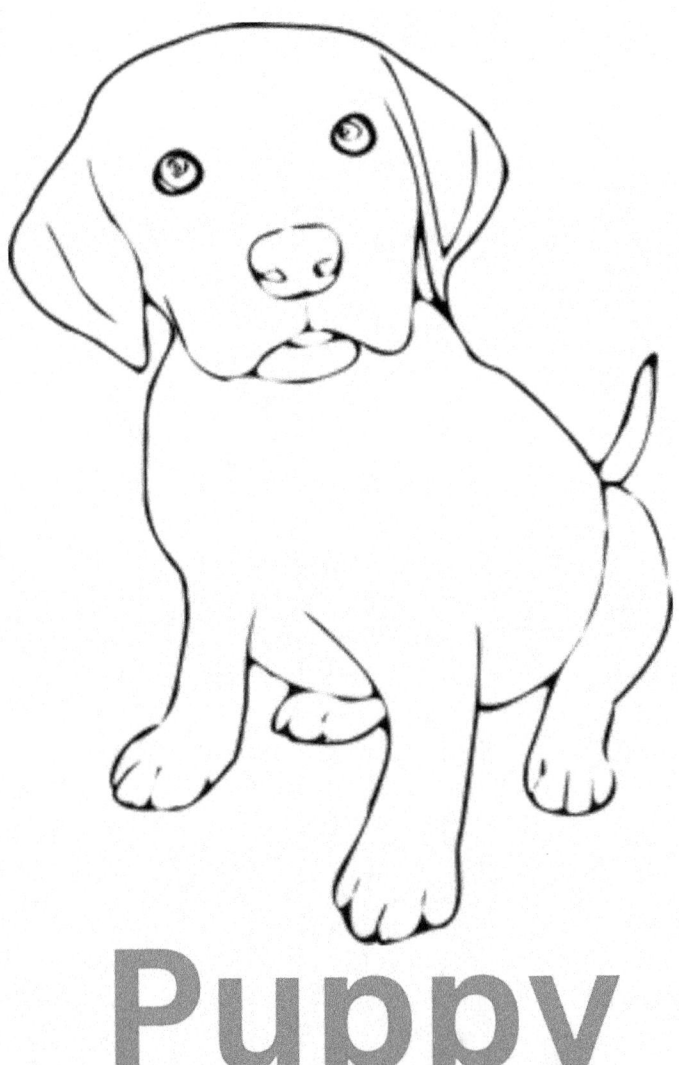

Puppy

● Brown

● Blue   Color the
                      Puppy with
● Yellow   these colors

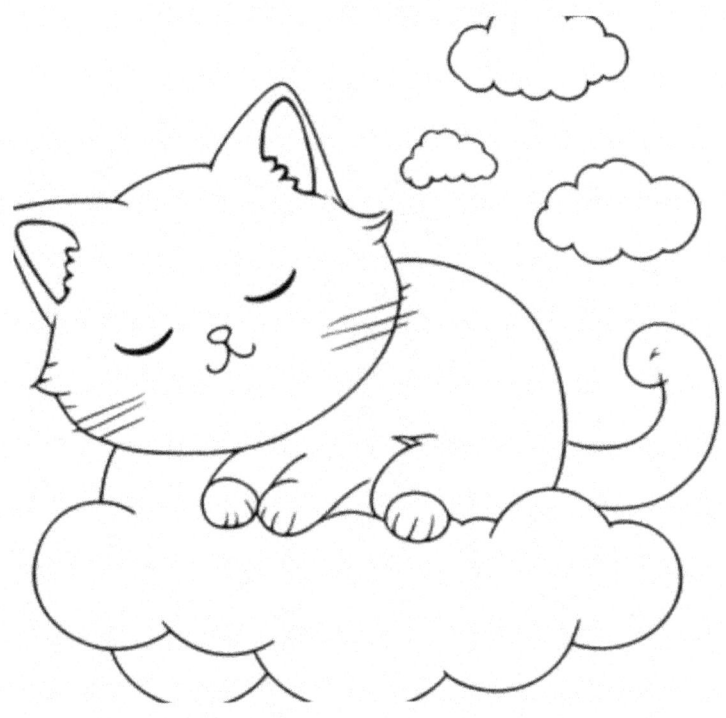

Kitten

Blue

Orange

Yellow

Color the Kitten
with these
colors

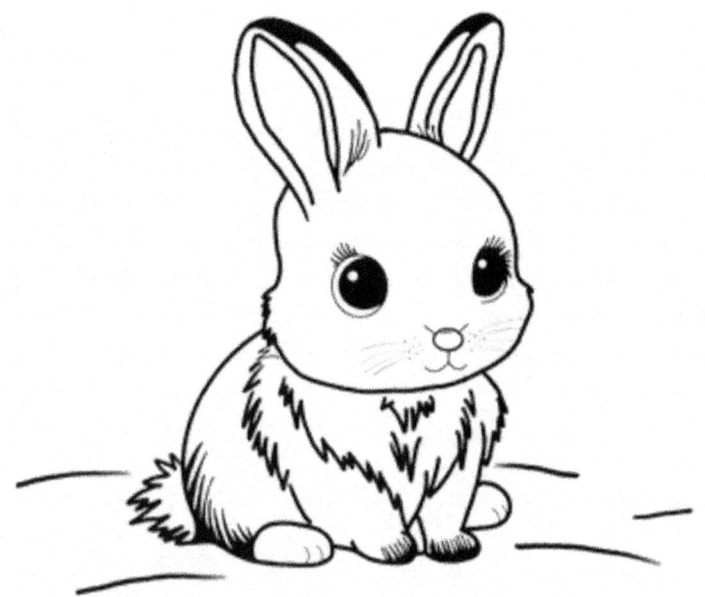

Bunny

Blue

Orange

Green

Color the
Bunny with
these colors

GINDAN MEDIA

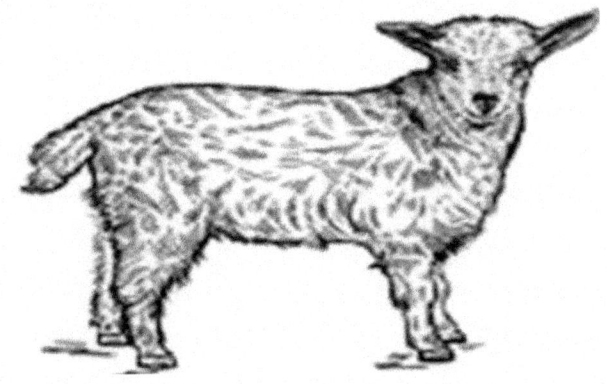

Kid

Blue

Grey

Pink

Color the Kid
with these
colors

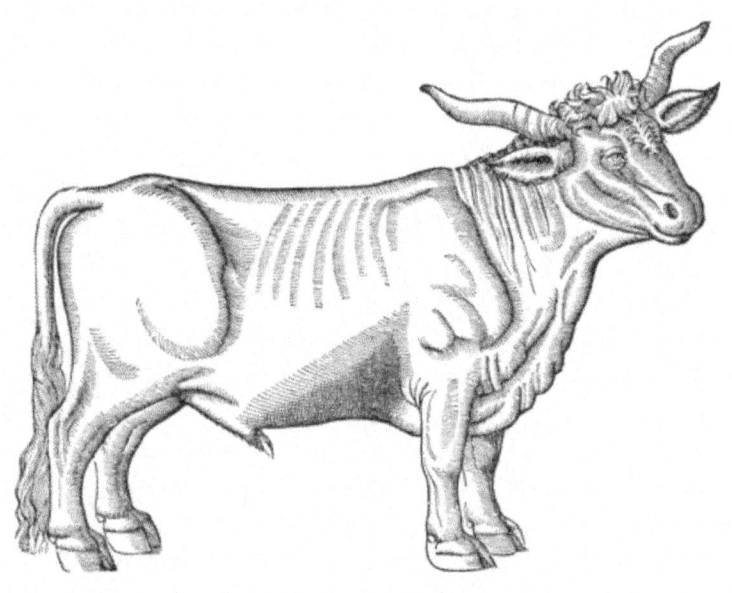

Ox

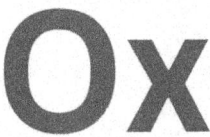

Brown

Grey

Pink

Color the Ox
with these
colors

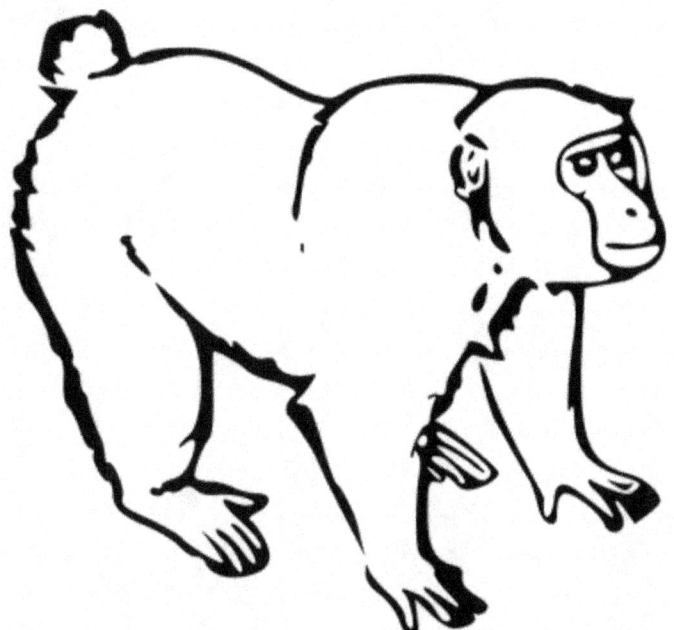

Monkey

- Pink
- Yellow
- Grey

Color the Monkey with these colors

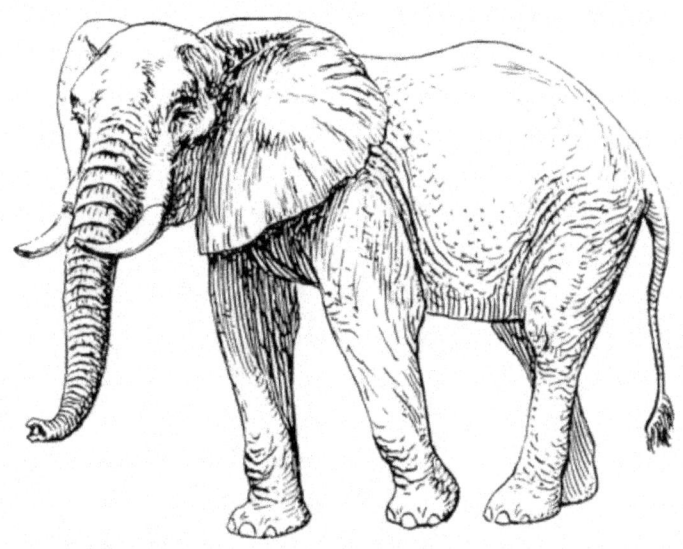

Eliphant

● Black

○ Yellow

● Grey

Color the
Eliphant with
these colors

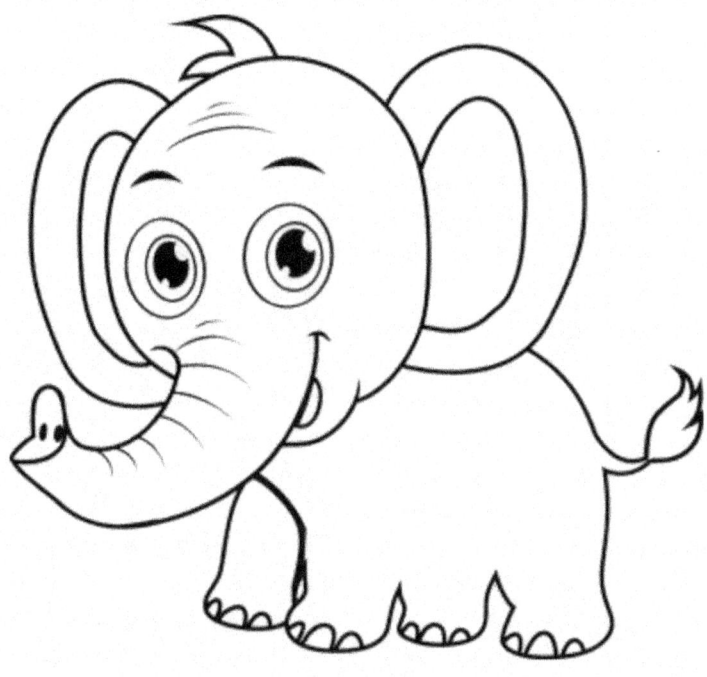

Calf

Pink

Yellow

Blue

Color the Calf
with these
colors

GINDAN MEDIA

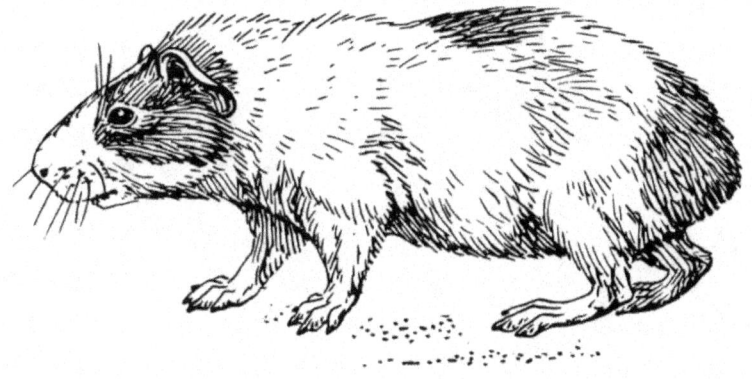

Guinea pig

● Pink

● Orange

● Black

Color the
guinea pig with
these colors

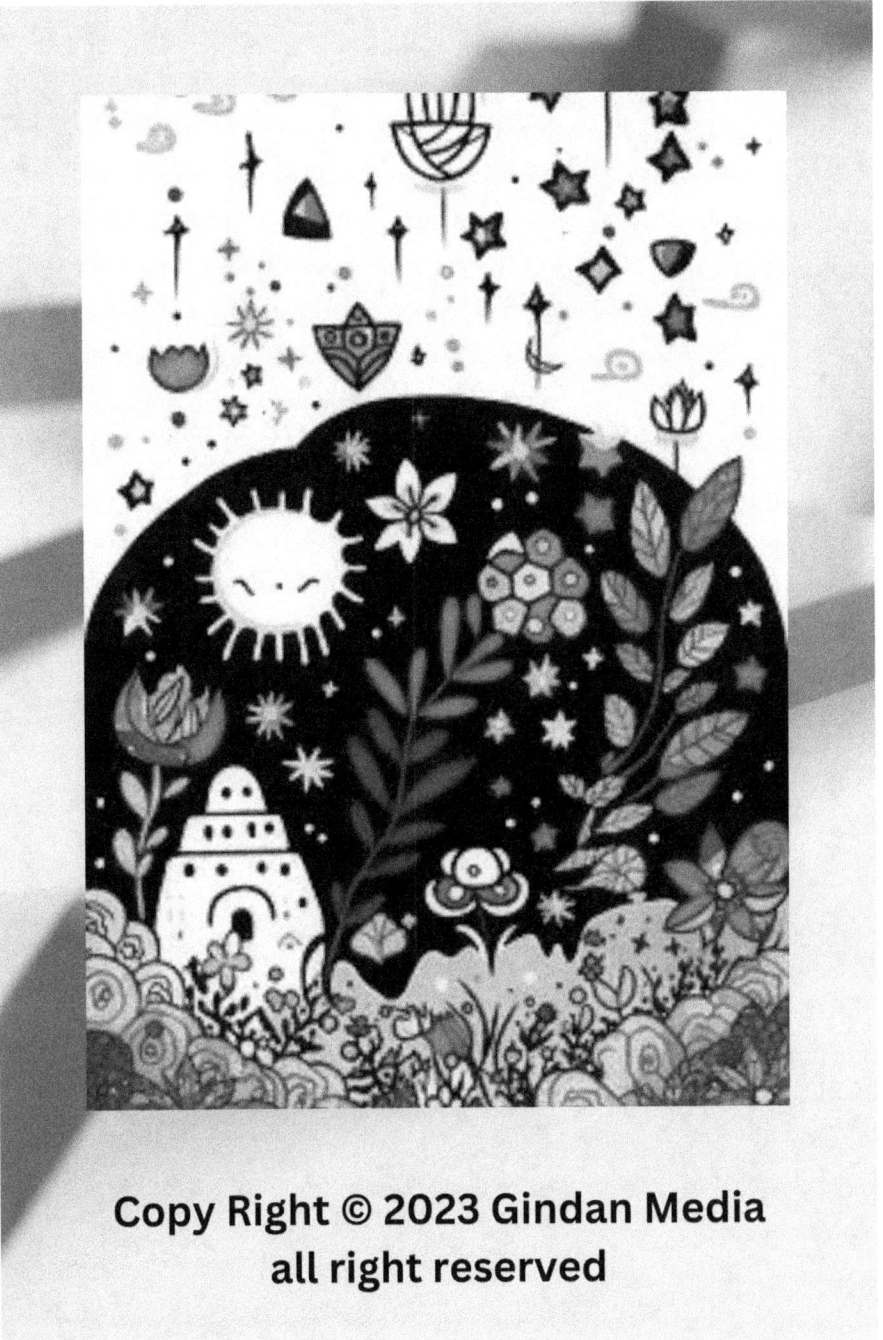

www.ingramcontent.com/pod-product-compliance
Lightning Source LLC
Chambersburg PA
CBHW070751220526
45467CB00018B/1938